# *Classic*
# VEGETARIAN

# *Classic*
# VEGETARIAN

*Appetizing dishes for every occasion*

FOREWORD BY
SARAH BROWN

HERMES
HOUSE

This edition published in 1998 by Hermes House

© 1996 Anness Publishing Limited

Hermes House is an imprint of
Anness Publishing Limited
Hermes House, 88-89 Blackfriars Road
London SE1 8HA

ISBN 1-84038-013-6

*Publisher* Joanna Lorenz
*Senior Cookery Editor* Linda Fraser
*Cookery Editor* Anne Hildyard
*Designer* Nigel Partridge
*Illustrations* Madeleine David
*Photographers* Karl Adamson, Steve Baxter, James Duncan and Michael Michaels
*Recipes* Alex Barker, Roz Denny, Christine France, Annie Nichols and Steven Wheeler
*Food for photography* Carole Handslip, Wendy Lee and Jane Stevenson
*Stylists* Madeleine Brehaut, Hilary Guy, Blake Minton and Kirsty Rawlings
*Jacket photography* Amanda Heywood

Typeset by MC Typeset Ltd, Rochester, Kent
Printed and bound in Singapore
3  5  7  9  10  8  6  4

For all recipes, quantities are given in both metric and imperial measures, and, where appropriate,
measures are also given in standard cups and spoons. Follow one set, but not a mixture,
because they are not interchangeable.

Pictures on frontispiece: Horizon International Images

# Contents

*Foreword 6*

*Introduction 8*

*Starters 10*

*Main Courses 16*

*Side Dishes 34*

*Pasta, Rice and Pizzas 40*

*Desserts 56*

*Index 64*

# FOREWORD

I became a vegetarian about twenty years ago when I was running a wholefood shop. From the very beginning I experimented with the ingredients I stocked, creating recipes and eventually selling food in my shop. So many people liked the results that I soon opened a restaurant, later sharing my recipes with an even wider public when I became a cookery writer. At that time vegetarian food hardly qualified as a cuisine. Many people viewed a vegetarian meal as something that consisted of a few vegetables and a space on the plate where the meat should have been!

During the last decade or so, vegetarian food has really come into its own. It is now seen as a cuisine in its own right, as this lovely book of classic recipes shows.

I have always drawn on ideas from around the world to create interesting recipes, so am pleased that *Classic Vegetarian* does exactly that. You can travel to Thailand and Italy and the Middle East without ever leaving your kitchen. Fresh herbs and exotic seasonings add an authentic note to many of the dishes.

The versatility of vegetarian food is amply illustrated by recipes for every occasion, from nutritious family meals to sophisticated suggestions for celebrations. If you are new to vegetarian cooking, look out for the useful Cook's Tips, which help you save time, offer hints on preparation or suggest different ways of adapting the recipe to suit your own requirements.

For anyone who is still worried about how to fill that space on the plate, this book provides plenty of food for thought. It is packed with good classic recipes, which use a wide variety of healthy ingredients, to produce dishes that are full of flavour, easy to make, and based on sound nutritional principles.

SARAH BROWN

# INTRODUCTION

This book celebrates the variety, versatility and sheer enjoyment offered by a vegetarian diet. The old image of meat-free meals as dull but worthy has long since disintegrated, and today's vegetarian meals are fresh, light and appetizing. Nor do you have to be a practising vegetarian to enjoy them: the increasing emphasis on healthy eating means that more and more families sit down several times a week to a meal of pasta or rice with vegetables or a cheese sauce, and the fact that meat does not feature is incidental rather than intentional. Few restaurant menus fail to feature a vegetarian dish, and whereas this was once invariably some sort of vegetable lasagne, the trend now is to offer more exciting and innovative dishes. Green Lentils with Sweet Onions; Broccoli and Chestnut Terrine; Leek and Stilton Samosas – delicious new ideas like these are featured in

*Purple-tipped globe artichokes ready to harvest (left), a rich variety of fresh vegetables beautifully displayed (above) and a colourful show of wonderful flavouring ingredients, including fresh herbs, chillies, root ginger and spices*

this contemporary collection.

A vegetarian diet can provide all the nutrients required for glowing good health, but it is important that meals be balanced to provide sufficient protein. Meat and fish are first-class or complete protein foods, containing all the essential amino acids the body needs for growth and repair. For lacto-vegetarians, protein sources include cereals, nuts, pulses, eggs, milk and cheese, none of which is a complete protein food in itself. To make up such deficiencies as there are, it is important to combine several sources of protein. Combining pulses (a good source of second-class protein) with a grain food, helps to redress the balance, especially if the meal also includes vegetables. This balance occurs naturally in many classic vegetarian dishes.

Wheat is probably the grain most commonly consumed. It comes in many different forms, from whole grain to milled flour. Wholewheat grain, once soaked, can be eaten in the same way as rice. Cracked wheat is the whole grain cracked between rollers, whereas bulgur (bulghur) is cracked wheat that has been hulled and steamed. Both grains can play a useful role in a vegetarian diet. Semolina, made from the starchy part of the grain, is used for gnocchi and couscous. Pasta, bread, cakes and biscuits contain wheat flour, and it is also used as a thickener in cooking.

Other grains include rice in all its varieties, rye kernels and barley, which is often added to soups and stews. Oats in various forms are invaluable for porridge, crumble toppings, in cakes and biscuits and for adding to savoury dishes. Corn comes in various forms, including hominy (dried corn used in savoury dishes) and cornmeal (ground white or yellow corn used for American cornbread and tortillas). In Italy, yellow cornmeal is called polenta and is used to make the dish of the same name.

Tofu, or soya bean curd, should not be overlooked as it is an excellent source of protein. Made from pressed, puréed soya beans, it is an important ingredient in oriental cooking.

Whether you are an established vegetarian, a recent convert to this way of eating or a cook who wants to introduce more meat-free dishes into a healthy eating plan, *Classic Vegetarian* will provide endless inspiration for many marvellous meals.

# WATERCRESS AND ORANGE SOUP

This is a very healthy and refreshing soup, which is just as good served hot or chilled. It freezes well – transfer to a freezer container before adding the cream.

### INGREDIENTS
*1 large onion, chopped*
*15ml/1 tbsp olive oil*
*2 bunches watercress*
*grated rind and juice of 1 large orange*
*1 vegetable stock cube*
*150ml/¼ pint/⅔ cup single cream*
*10ml/2 tsp cornflour*
*salt and ground black pepper*
*a little thick cream or yogurt, to garnish*
*4 orange wedges, to serve*

*SERVES 4*

COOK'S TIP
Wash the watercress only if really necessary; it is often very clean.

1 Place the onion in the oil in a large saucepan and cook gently, stirring occasionally, for 5 minutes until softened. Trim and discard any large stalks from the watercress, then add the watercress to the onion. Cover the pan and cook the watercress for about 5 minutes, until wilted and softened.

2 Add the orange rind and juice. Dissolve the stock cube in 600ml/1 pint/2½ cups water, then add to the pan. Cover and simmer for 10–15 minutes. While the soup is cooking, blend the cream with the cornflour.

3 Transfer to a food processor or blender and blend the soup thoroughly, then pour through a sieve if you like. Return to the pan, add the cream and cornflour mixture, and seasoning to taste.

4 Bring the soup gently back to the boil, stirring until just slightly thickened. Check the seasoning and serve the soup with a swirl of cream or yogurt, and a wedge of orange to squeeze in at the last moment.

# GARLIC BAKED TOMATOES

I f you can find them, use Italian plum tomatoes, which have a warm, slightly sweet flavour. For large numbers of people you could use whole cherry tomatoes, tossed several times during cooking.

### INGREDIENTS
*40g/1½oz/3 tbsp unsalted butter*
*1 large garlic clove, crushed*
*5ml/1 tsp finely grated orange rind*
*4 firm plum tomatoes, or 2 large beef tomatoes*
*salt and ground black pepper*
*fresh basil leaves, to garnish*

### SERVES 4

---

### COOK'S TIP
Garlic butter is well worth keeping in the freezer. Make it up as above, or omit the orange rind and add some chopped fresh parsley. Freeze in thick slices or chunks ready to use, or roll into a sausage shape and wrap in foil, then cut into slices when partly defrosted.

---

1 In a small bowl, soften the butter with a wooden spoon and blend with the garlic, orange rind and seasoning. Chill the butter for a few minutes.

2 Preheat the oven to 200°C/400°F/Gas 6. Halve the tomatoes crossways and trim the bases so they stand firmly.

3 Place the tomatoes in an ovenproof dish and spread the garlic butter equally over each tomato half.

4 Bake the garlic tomatoes in the oven for 15–25 minutes, depending on the size of the tomato halves, until they are just tender. Serve the tomatoes, garnished with the fresh basil leaves.

# RICE AND CHEESE CROQUETTES

A lthough you can use leftover cooked rice in this dish, freshly cooked rice is easier to work with. The garlicky mayonnaise, aïoli, makes a good dip for crudités too.

### INGREDIENTS
*115g/4oz/½ cup long grain rice, cooked*
*2 eggs, lightly beaten*
*75g/3oz mozzarella cheese, grated*
*50g/2oz/½ cup fine breadcrumbs*
*salt and ground black pepper*
*oil, for frying*
*dill sprigs, to garnish*

### FOR THE AÏOLI
*1 egg yolk*
*few drops of lemon juice or vinegar*
*1 large garlic clove, crushed*
*250ml/8fl oz/1 cup olive oil*

*MAKES ABOUT 16*

1 Drain the cooked rice thoroughly and allow to cool slightly, then mix in the eggs, cheese and seasoning.

2 Mould the rice mixture into 16 equal-size balls and coat in breadcrumbs, pressing on the crumbs well. Chill for 20 minutes.

3 Meanwhile, to make the aïoli, put the egg yolk, lemon juice or vinegar, garlic and seasoning into a bowl and beat together. Gradually whisk in sufficient oil, adding it drop by drop and whisking well between each addition, to give a thick, glossy mayonnaise. Cover and chill before serving.

4 Heat the oil in a frying pan until almost hazy, then cook the rice balls, in two batches, for 4–5 minutes each, or until crisp and golden all over. Drain the rice balls on kitchen paper and keep warm until required (or reheat in a hot oven) before garnishing with dill sprigs and serving with the aïoli.

# LEEK AND STILTON SAMOSAS

hese three-cornered parcels make great party nibbles. You can prepare them well in advance and freeze them ready to cook.

### INGREDIENTS
*2 leeks, sliced*
*30ml/2 tbsp milk*
*15ml/1 tbsp orange juice*
*75g/3oz/¾ cup Stilton cheese, crumbled or diced*
*8 sheets filo pastry*
*25g/1oz/2 tbsp butter, melted*
*ground black pepper*
*fresh coriander sprigs, to garnish*

*MAKES 16*

---

### COOK'S TIP
Filo pastry dries out very quickly and then becomes impossible to work with. Cover with a damp dish towel and take out one sheet at a time.

---

1 Cook the leeks very gently in the milk and orange juice for about 8–10 minutes, until really soft, then season with pepper. Allow the leek mixture to cool slightly before stirring in the Stilton.

2 Preheat the oven to 200°C/400°F/Gas 6. Lay one sheet of pastry flat, brush it with butter and cut in half to make a long oblong strip. Place one-sixteenth of the leek and Stilton mixture in the bottom right-hand corner. Fold the corner point up and over the filling towards the left edge to form a triangular shape.

3 Next, fold the bottom left-hand point up to give a straight bottom edge to the pastry sheet, then fold the pastry triangle over to the right and then up again, so that the filling is completely enclosed. Continue folding up the sheet of pastry and tuck the top flap underneath. Brush with a little butter and place on a baking sheet.

4 Repeat this process for the rest of the pastry and filling mixture, to make about 16 samosas in all.

5 Bake the samosas for 10-15 minutes, until golden brown and crisp. Serve hot, as a snack, garnished with coriander sprigs as a starter, or hand round as a nibble with drinks.

# SPINACH AND RICOTTA CONCHIGLIE

Large pasta shells are designed to hold a variety of delicious stuffings. Few are more pleasing than this mixture of spinach and ricotta cheese.

INGREDIENTS

*350g/12oz large conchiglie*
*450ml/¾ pint/1⅞ cup passata or*
*tomato pulp*
*275g/10oz frozen chopped spinach,*
*defrosted*
*50g/2oz/1 cup crustless white*
*bread, crumbled*
*120ml/4fl oz/½ cup milk*
*60ml/4 tbsp olive oil*
*225g/8oz/2¼ cups ricotta cheese*
*pinch of nutmeg*
*1 garlic clove, crushed*
*2.5ml/½ tsp black olive paste (optional)*
*25g/1oz/¼ cup freshly grated*
*Parmesan cheese*
*25g/1oz/2 tbsp pine nuts*
*salt and ground black pepper*

SERVES 4

COOK'S TIP
Choose a large saucepan when cooking pasta and give it an occasional stir to prevent the shapes from sticking together.

1 Bring a large saucepan of salted water to the boil. Toss in the pasta and cook for about 12 minutes, or until *al dente*. Refresh the pasta under cold water, drain and reserve until needed.

2 Pour the passata or tomato pulp into a sieve over a bowl and strain to thicken. Place the spinach in another sieve and press out any excess liquid with a spoon.

3 Place the bread, milk and 45ml/3 tbsp of the oil in a food processor or blender and combine. Add the spinach and ricotta and season with salt, pepper and nutmeg.

4 Combine the passata or tomato pulp with the garlic, the remaining olive oil and olive paste, if using. Spread the sauce evenly over the bottom of an ovenproof dish. Spoon the spinach mixture into a piping bag fitted with a large plain nozzle and fill the pasta shapes (alternatively, fill with a spoon). Arrange the pasta shapes over the sauce.

5 Preheat a moderate grill. Heat the pasta through in a medium/190°C/375°F/ Gas 5 oven for about 10 minutes. Scatter with Parmesan cheese and pine nuts, and grill until the cheese is browned.

# VEGGIE BURGERS

hese simple burgers are quick to make and cook, and are ideal for a snack or light meal. Chutneys or pickles, especially home-made ones, are a good accompaniment.

## INGREDIENTS
*115g/4oz cup mushrooms, finely chopped*
*1 small onion, chopped*
*1 small courgette, chopped*
*1 carrot, chopped*
*25g/1oz unsalted peanuts or cashews*
*115g/4oz/2 cups fresh breadcrumbs*
*30ml/2 tbsp chopped fresh parsley*
*5ml/1 tsp yeast extract*
*fine oatmeal or flour, for shaping*
*oil, for frying*
*salt and ground black pepper*
*crisp salad, to serve*

### SERVES 4

1 Cook the mushrooms in a non-stick pan without oil, stirring, for 8–10 minutes to remove all the moisture.

2 Process the onion, courgette, carrot and nuts in a food processor or blender until beginning to bind together.

3 Stir in the mushrooms, breadcrumbs, parsley, yeast extract and seasoning to taste. With the oatmeal or flour, shape into four burgers (*left*) and chill until firm.

4 Cook the burgers in a non-stick frying pan with very little oil for 8–10 minutes, turning once, until golden brown. Serve hot with a crisp salad.

# THAI TOFU CURRY

**T**hai cooking brings together elements from Malay, Chinese and Indian cuisine. The favourite Thai flavourings used in this recipe enhance the tofu curry perfectly.

### INGREDIENTS
*2 × 200g/7oz cartons tofu, cubed*
*30ml/2 tbsp light soy sauce*
*30ml/2 tbsp groundnut oil*

### FOR THE SPICE PASTE
*1 small onion, chopped*
*2 fresh green chillies, seeded*
*and chopped*
*2 garlic cloves, chopped*
*5ml/1 tsp grated fresh root ginger*
*5ml/1 tsp grated lime rind*
*juice of 1 lime or small lemon*
*10ml/2 tsp coriander seeds, crushed*
*10ml/2 tsp cumin seeds, crushed*
*45ml/3 tbsp chopped fresh coriander*
*15ml/1 tbsp soy sauce*
*5ml/1 tsp sugar*
*25g/1oz creamed coconut, dissolved in*
*150ml/¼ pint/⅔ cup boiling water*
*thin slices of fresh red chilli and*
*lime slices, to garnish*
*rice, to serve*

### SERVES 4

1 Toss the tofu cubes in soy sauce and leave to marinate for 15 minutes or so while you prepare the spice paste.

2 Combine the onion, chillies, garlic, ginger, lime rind and juice, coriander and cumin seeds, fresh coriander, soy sauce, sugar and coconut in a blender.

3 Heat the oil in a wok or large frying pan until quite hot. Drain the tofu cubes, add to the wok and stir-fry for 5–8 minutes over a high heat, until they are well browned on all sides and just firm. Lift out with a slotted spoon and drain on kitchen paper.

4 Wipe out the wok. Pour in the spice paste and stir well over a moderate heat. Return the tofu to the wok and mix it into the spice paste, stirring until it is warmed through. Garnish with the red chilli and lime slices and serve with rice.

# LEEK AND BROCCOLI TARTLETS

Tasty and attractive, these little tartlets with crisp vegetables in a cheese-flavoured pastry are also ideal served as a starter on their own.

### INGREDIENTS
*175g/6oz/1½ cups plain flour, sifted*
*115g/4oz/½ cup butter*
*25g/1oz finely grated pecorino or Parmesan cheese*
*60–90ml/4–6 tbsp cold water*
*flour, for rolling*
*2 small leeks, sliced*
*75g/3oz tiny broccoli florets*
*150ml/¼ pint/⅔ cup milk*
*2 eggs*
*30ml/2 tbsp double cream*
*few pinches of ground mace*
*salt and ground black pepper*
*15g/½oz flaked almonds, toasted, to garnish*

*SERVES 4*

### COOK'S TIP
Cook and freeze the tartlet cases, ready for use at any time. They only need 15 minutes defrosting. Use other colourful, crunchy vegetables when they are in season.

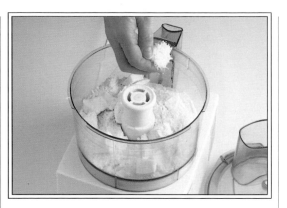

1 Blend together the flour, butter and cheese in a food processor or blender to give a fine crumb consistency. Add salt and just enough water to bring the pastry together into a ball. Chill for 15 minutes.

2 Preheat the oven to 190°C/375°F/Gas 5. Roll out the pastry on a floured surface and use to line four 10cm/4in tartlet tins. Line the pastry cases with greaseproof paper and fill with baking beans. Bake the tartlets for 15 minutes, then remove the paper and beans and cook for a further 5 minutes to dry out the bases.

3 To make the filling, place the leeks and broccoli in a saucepan with the milk and simmer for 2–3 minutes. Strain the milk into a small bowl and whisk in the eggs, cream, mace and seasoning.

4 Arrange the leeks and broccoli in the pastry cases and pour over the egg mixture. Bake for 20 minutes, or until the filling is just firm. Sprinkle the tartlets with the toasted almonds before serving.

# BAKED AUBERGINE SLICES

**A**n unusual way to prepare and cook aubergines, this dish is substantial enough to be served as a light lunch, although it can also be served as an accompaniment to pasta dishes.

### INGREDIENTS
*45–60ml/3–4 tbsp olive oil*
*1 large aubergine*
*2 large tomatoes, thickly sliced*
*few fresh basil leaves, shredded*
*115g/4oz mozzarella cheese, sliced*
*salt and ground black pepper*
*fresh basil sprig, to garnish*

*SERVES 4*

1 Preheat the oven to 190°C/375°F/Gas 5. Brush a baking sheet with a little oil. Trim the aubergine and cut lengthways into slices about 5mm/¼in thick. Arrange the slices on the greased sheet.

2 Brush the aubergine slices liberally with the oil and season with salt and pepper. Arrange the tomato, basil leaves and cheese slices alternately on top of each aubergine slice. Brush lightly with oil.

3 Sprinkle with ground black pepper and bake for about 15 minutes, or until the aubergine is tender and the cheese is bubbling and golden. Serve the slices garnished with the fresh basil sprig.

22

# SPINACH AND POTATO GALETTE

C reamy layers of potato, spinach and herbs make a warming supper dish. Galette is only one of the many French names for a type of tart.

INGREDIENTS
*900g/2lb large potatoes*
*450g/1lb fresh spinach*
*2 eggs*
*400g/14oz/1¾ cups low-fat cream cheese*
*15ml/1 tbsp whole-grain mustard*
*45ml/3 tbsp chopped fresh herbs, such as*
*chives, parsley, chervil or sorrel*
*salt and ground black pepper*
*salad, to serve*

SERVES 6

1 Preheat the oven to 180°C/350°F/Gas 4. Line a deep 23cm/9in cake tin with non-stick baking paper. Place the potatoes in a large pan, cover with cold water, bring to the boil and cook for 10 minutes. Drain and cool slightly before slicing thinly.

2 Wash the spinach and place in a large pan with only the water that is clinging to the leaves. Cover and cook, stirring once, until it has just wilted. Drain well in a sieve and squeeze out all of the excess moisture. Chop the spinach finely.

3 Beat the eggs with the cream cheese and mustard, then stir in the chopped spinach and fresh herbs.

4 Place a layer of the sliced potatoes in the lined tin, arranging them in concentric circles. Cover with a spoonful of the cream cheese mixture and spread out. Continue layering, seasoning with salt and pepper as you go, until all the potatoes and the cream-cheese mixture are used up. Cover the cake tin tightly with a piece of foil and place in a roasting tin.

5 Fill the roasting tin with enough boiling water to come halfway up the sides of the cake tin and bake for 45–50 minutes. Serve hot or cold with a salad.

# MIDDLE EASTERN VEGETABLE STEW

A spiced dish of mixed vegetables that can be served as a side-dish or as a main course. Mint and cumin are two of the most popular Middle Eastern flavourings.

### INGREDIENTS
*45ml/3 tbsp vegetable stock*
*1 green pepper, seeded and sliced*
*2 courgettes, sliced*
*2 carrots, sliced*
*2 celery sticks, sliced*
*2 potatoes, diced*
*400g/14oz can chopped tomatoes*
*5ml/1 tsp chilli powder*
*30ml/2 tbsp chopped fresh mint*
*15ml/1 tbsp ground cumin*
*400g/14oz can chick-peas, drained*
*salt and ground black pepper*
*fresh mint leaves, to garnish*

### SERVES 4–6

1 Pour the vegetable stock into a large flameproof casserole and heat until boiling, then add the sliced green pepper, courgettes, carrots and celery. Cook over a high heat for 2–3 minutes, stirring and turning often, until the vegetables are just beginning to soften.

2 Add the potatoes and tomatoes to the casserole, then season with the chilli powder, chopped mint and cumin. Add the chick-peas and stir to mix the vegetables and spices together, then bring to the boil

3 Reduce the heat, cover the casserole, and simmer for 30 minutes, or until all the vegetables are tender and cooked through. Season to taste and serve hot, garnished with mint leaves.

### COOK'S TIP
Chick-peas are traditional in this type of Middle Eastern dish, but if you prefer, red kidney beans or haricot beans can be used instead.

# APPLE, ONION AND GRUYERE TART

T he grated apple adds a subtle flavour to this flan filling. Other hard cheeses, such as Cheddar or Lancashire may be used instead of Gruyère.

### INGREDIENTS
*250g/8oz/2 cups plain flour*
*1.5ml/¼ tsp mustard powder*
*75g/3oz/6 tbsp soft margarine*
*75g/3oz/6 tbsp finely grated*
*Gruyère cheese*
*30ml/2 tbsp water*
*crisp salad, to serve*

### FOR THE FILLING
*25g/1oz/2 tbsp butter*
*1 large onion, finely chopped*
*2 small eating apples, peeled and grated*
*2 large eggs*
*150ml/¼ pint/⅔ cup double cream*
*1.5ml/¼ tsp dried mixed herbs*
*2.5ml/½ tsp mustard powder*
*115g/4oz Gruyère cheese*
*salt and ground black pepper*

### SERVES 4–6

1 To make the pastry, sift the flour, salt and mustard into a large bowl. Rub in the margarine and cheese until the mixture forms soft crumbs. Add the water and mix to a dough. Chill, covered, for 30 minutes.

2 Meanwhile, to make the filling, melt the butter in a pan, add the onion and cook gently for 10 minutes, stirring occasionally, until softened but not browned. Stir in the apple and cook for 2–3 minutes, then remove from the heat and leave to cool.

3 Preheat the oven to 200°C/400°F/Gas 6. Roll out the pastry and use to line a lightly greased 20cm/8in springform tin. Chill for 20 minutes. Line the pastry case with greaseproof paper and fill with baking beans. Bake for 20 minutes.

4 Beat together the eggs, cream, herbs, mustard and seasoning. Grate three-quarters of the cheese and stir into the egg mixture, then slice the remaining cheese and set aside. When the pastry is cooked, remove the paper and beans and pour in the egg mixture.

5 Arrange the sliced cheese over the top. Reduce the oven heat to 190°C/375°F/Gas 5. Return the tart to the oven and cook for 20 minutes, until the filling is just firm. Serve hot or warm with a salad.

# GREEN LENTILS WITH SWEET ONIONS

A delicious, wholesome dish with a sweet flavour, topped with crunchy cashews for added bite. The dark blue-green Puy lentils from France would be a good choice.

### INGREDIENTS
*30ml/2 tbsp sunflower oil*
*1 small onion, chopped*
*2 garlic cloves, crushed*
*175g/6oz/1 cup green lentils*
*600ml/1 pint/2½ cups vegetable stock*
*150ml/¼ pint/⅔ cup red wine*
*5ml/1 tsp chopped fresh sage, or a pinch of dried sage*
*225g/8oz button onions, peeled*
*50g/2oz/4 tbsp butter*
*50g/2oz/4 tbsp soft light brown sugar*
*salt and ground black pepper*
*25g/1oz/½ salted cashews and thyme sprigs, to garnish*

### SERVES 3–4

1 Heat the oil in a flameproof casserole and fry the onion and garlic until soft. Add the lentils (*left*) and fry gently for 3 minutes.

2 Stir in the stock, red wine, sage and seasoning. Bring to the boil. Cover and simmer gently for 20 minutes, stirring occasionally, until the lentils are tender. Add more liquid if necessary.

3 Meanwhile, in a small frying pan, gently fry the onions with the butter and sugar for 5–7 minutes, until the sugar begins to caramelize and the onions are just tender. Stir occasionally.

4 Serve the lentils sprinkled with the cashews, garnished with thyme sprigs, and accompanied by the onions.

# MUSHROOM POPOVERS

Individual Yorkshire puddings with a quick-and-easy mushroom filling will be a popular choice with the whole family.

### INGREDIENTS
*1 egg*
*115g/4oz/1 cup plain flour*
*300ml/½ pint/1¼ cups milk*
*pinch of salt*
*oil, for greasing*

### FOR THE FILLING
*15ml/1 tbsp sunflower oil*
*115g/4oz mushrooms, sliced*
*few drops of lemon juice*
*10ml/2 tsp chopped fresh
parsley or thyme*
*¼ red pepper, seeded and chopped*
*salt and ground black pepper*
*shredded fresh basil and fresh
basil leaves, to garnish*

### SERVES 4

1 To make the popovers, whisk the egg and flour together and gradually add a little milk to blend, then whisk in the rest of the milk to make a smooth batter. Add a pinch of salt and leave the batter to stand for at least 10–20 minutes.

2 Preheat the oven to 190°C/375°F/Gas 5. Pour a little oil into the base of eight Yorkshire pudding tins and heat through in the oven for 4–5 minutes. Add the batter to the hot tins and cook for 20 minutes, or until well risen and crispy.

### COOK'S TIP
For perfect batter, it is important that both the fat and the oven are very hot otherwise the batter will be heavy, tough or soggy. When a batter doesn't rise properly, the mixture is probably too thin.

3 Meanwhile, to make the filling, heat the oil and sauté the mushrooms with the lemon juice, herbs and seasoning until most of the liquid has evaporated. Add the red pepper at the last minute so that it keeps its crunch. Taste for seasoning.

4 Spoon the mushroom filling into the hot popover cases, scatter over the basil and serve immediately.

# BROCCOLI AND CHESTNUT TERRINE

his attractive terrine, which is equally good hot or cold, makes a splendid main course for a dinner party. It is also perfect for a picnic.

### INGREDIENTS
*450g/1lb broccoli, cut into small florets*
*225g/8oz cooked chestnuts,*
*roughly chopped*
*50g/2oz/1 cup fresh wholemeal*
*breadcrumbs*
*60ml/4 tbsp low-fat natural yogurt*
*30ml/2 tbsp Parmesan cheese,*
*finely grated*
*salt, grated nutmeg and ground*
*black pepper*
*2 eggs, beaten*
*new potatoes and salad, to serve*

*SERVES 4–6*

1 Preheat the oven to 180°C/350°F/Gas 4. Line a 900g/2lb loaf tin with non-stick baking paper.

2 Blanch or steam the broccoli for 3–4 minutes until just tender. Drain well. Reserve a quarter of the smallest florets and chop the rest finely.

3 Place the chopped chestnuts, with the breadcrumbs, yogurt and Parmesan in a large bowl and season to taste with salt, nutmeg and pepper. Fold in the chopped broccoli, the reserved florets and the beaten eggs and stir until thoroughly combined.

4 Spoon the broccoli mixture into the tin. Place in a roasting tin and pour in boiling water to come halfway up the sides of the loaf tin. Bake for 20–25 minutes. Remove from the oven and tip out on to a plate. Slice and serve with potatoes and salad.

# CHICK-PEAS AND ARTICHOKES AU GRATIN

**A** very quick and extremely tasty dish, with an unusual combination of flavours that will impress friends and family alike.

### INGREDIENTS
*400g/14oz can chick-peas, drained*
*400g/14oz can black-eyed beans, drained*
*137g/4½oz jar artichoke antipasti (or canned artichoke hearts, chopped, plus a little olive oil)*
*1 red pepper, seeded and chopped*
*1 garlic clove, crushed*
*15ml/1 tbsp chopped fresh parsley*
*5ml/1 tsp lemon juice*
*150ml/¼ pint/⅔ cup soured cream*
*1 egg yolk*
*50g/2oz/½ cup grated Cheddar cheese*
*salt and ground black pepper*

### SERVES 4

1 Preheat the oven to 180°C/350°F/Gas 4. Mix together the chick-peas, black-eyed beans, artichoke antipasti or artichoke hearts and red pepper.

2 Stir in as much of the dressing from the antipasti, or oil if using artichoke hearts, as necessary to moisten the mixture. Stir in the garlic, parsley, lemon juice, and season.

3 Mix together the soured cream, egg yolk, cheese and seasoning. Spoon evenly over the vegetables (*left*) and bake for 25–30 minutes, or until the top is golden brown.

# BROCCOLI-CAULIFLOWER GRATIN

roccoli and cauliflower make an attractive combination, and this sauce is much lighter than the classic cheese sauce.

### INGREDIENTS
*1 small cauliflower, about 250g/9oz*
*1 small head broccoli, about 250g/9oz*
*salt*
*120ml/4fl oz/½ cup natural low-fat yogurt*
*115g/4oz/1 cup Cheddar cheese, grated*
*5ml/1 tsp whole-grain mustard*
*30ml/2 tbsp wholemeal breadcrumbs*
*salt and ground black pepper*

### SERVES 4

---

### COOK'S TIP
When preparing the cauliflower and broccoli, discard the tougher part of the stalks, then break the florets into even-size pieces, so they cook evenly.

1 Break the cauliflower and broccoli into florets and cook in lightly salted boiling water for 8–10 minutes, until just tender. Drain well and transfer to a flameproof dish

2 In a bowl, mix together the yogurt, cheese and mustard, then season the mixture with pepper and spoon evenly over the cauliflower and broccoli.

3 Sprinkle the breadcrumbs over the top of the sauce and place the dish under a preheated hot grill and cook until golden brown and bubbling. Serve hot.

# LEMON CARROT SALAD

**E**njoy this tangy, colourful and refreshing salad at any time. If you like, add a sprinkling of toasted sesame seeds just before serving.

### INGREDIENTS
*450g/1lb baby carrots*
*grated rind and juice of ½ lemon*
*15ml/1 tbsp soft light brown sugar*
*60ml/4 tbsp sunflower oil*
*5ml/1 tsp hazelnut or sesame oil*
*5ml/1 tsp chopped fresh oregano, and a*
*fresh oregano sprig, to garnish*
*salt and ground black pepper*

*SERVES 4–6*

---

### COOK'S TIP
Other root vegetables can be used in this salad. For instance, you could try replacing half of the carrot with swede, or use celeriac or kohlrabi instead.

---

1 Finely grate the carrots and place them in a large bowl. Stir in the lemon rind, 15–30ml/1–2 tbsp of the lemon juice, the sugar and oils, and mix well.

2 Add more lemon juice and seasoning to taste, then sprinkle on the oregano, toss lightly and leave the salad for 1 hour before serving, garnished with the oregano sprig.

# CRISP FRUITY SALAD

C risp lettuce, tangy cheese, sweet grapes, crunchy pieces of apple and garlic croûtons make this an interesting and refreshing salad.

### INGREDIENTS
*½ Webb's lettuce*
*75g/3oz grapes, seeded and halved*
*50g/2oz/½ cup mature Cheddar cheese, grated*
*1 large eating apple, cored and thinly sliced*
*45ml/3 tbsp garlic croûtons, to garnish*

### FOR THE VINAIGRETTE
*15ml/1 tbsp French mustard*
*15ml/1 tbsp white wine vinegar*
*pinch of sugar*
*60ml/4 tbsp sunflower oil*
*salt and ground black pepper*

### SERVES 4

1 Tear the lettuce leaves into bite-size pieces and place in a salad bowl. Add the grapes, cheese and apple.

2 To make the vinaigrette dressing, put the mustard, vinegar, sugar and seasoning into a small bowl and whisk together with a fork to combine. Gradually add the oil, whisking to emulsify.

3 Pour the dressing over the salad *(left)*. Mix well and serve at once, sprinkled with garlic croûtons.

# WATERCRESS AND POTATO SALAD

New potatoes are equally delicious hot or cold, and this colourful, nutritious salad is an ideal way of making the most of them.

### INGREDIENTS
*450g/1lb small new potatoes, unpeeled*
*1 bunch watercress*
*225g/8oz/1½ cups cherry*
*tomatoes, halved*
*30ml/2 tbsp pumpkin seeds*
*45ml/3 tbsp low-fat fromage frais*
*15ml/1 tbsp cider vinegar*
*5ml/1 tsp brown sugar*
*salt and paprika*

### SERVES 4

### COOK'S TIP
If you are packing this salad for a picnic, take the dressing in the jar and toss in just before serving.

1 Cook the potatoes in lightly salted boiling water until just tender, then drain and leave to cool.

2 Put the potatoes, watercress, cherry tomatoes and pumpkin seeds into a bowl and toss together.

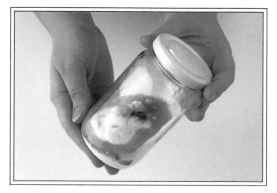

3 Place the fromage frais, vinegar, sugar, salt and paprika in a screw-top jar and shake well to mix. Pour the dressing over the salad just before serving.

### VARIATION
Potato salad is an essential part of summer eating, but there are endless ways to ring the changes to this simple recipe. The one essential is a good waxy salad potato, as freshly dug as possible – they taste so much better that way. Young spinach leaves or the peppery-flavoured rocket can be used instead of the watercress or you can use any combination of two, or all three of them. Soured cream can be used instead of fromage frais and balsamic vinegar with its more mellow flavour substituted for the cider vinegar.

# SPICY BAKED POTATOES

**B**aked potatoes are a universal favourite. Here, a combination of fresh ginger and warming aromatic spices add an unusual piquant flavour.

### INGREDIENTS
*2 large baking potatoes*
*5ml/1 tsp sunflower oil*
*1 small onion, finely chopped*
*2.5cm/1in piece fresh root ginger, grated*
*5ml/1 tsp ground cumin*
*5ml/1 tsp ground coriander*
*2.5ml/½ tsp ground turmeric*
*garlic salt, to taste*
*plain yogurt and fresh coriander sprigs, to serve*

### SERVES 2–4

1 Preheat the oven to 190°C/375°F/Gas 5. Prick the potatoes with a fork. Bake for 40 minutes, or until soft.

2 Cut the potatoes lengthways in half, scoop out the flesh and set aside on a plate. Heat the oil in a large non-stick frying pan, add the onion and sauté for a few minutes to soften.

3 Add the ginger, cumin, coriander and turmeric to the onion and stir over a low heat for about 2 minutes. Add the potato flesh and garlic salt, to taste, and stir to coat thoroughly with the spice mixture.

4 Cook the potato mixture for a further 2 minutes, stirring occasionally. Spoon the mixture back into the potato shells and top each potato with a spoonful of yogurt and a coriander sprig. Serve hot.

# STIR-FRIED FLORETS WITH HAZELNUTS

 rich hazelnut sauce transforms crunchy cauliflower and broccoli florets into a special vegetable dish.

### INGREDIENTS
*175g/6oz cauliflower, broken into florets*
*175g/6oz broccoli, broken into florets*
*15ml/1 tbsp sunflower oil*
*50g/2oz/½ cup hazelnuts, finely chopped*
*60ml/4 tbsp crème fraîche or*
*soured cream*
*salt and ground black pepper*
*chilli powder or finely chopped*
*red pepper, to garnish*

*SERVES 4*

1 Make sure the cauliflower and broccoli florets are all of a similar size. Heat the oil in a large frying pan or wok and toss the florets over a high heat for 1 minute.

2 Reduce the heat and continue to stir-fry for another 5 minutes, then add the hazelnuts and season to taste.

3 When the cauliflower and broccoli florets are crisp and nearly tender stir in the crème fraîche or soured cream and heat gently until the mixture is just warmed through. Serve the florets immediately, garnished with a fine sprinkling of chilli powder or finely chopped red pepper.

### COOK'S TIP
The crisper these florets are the better, so cook them just long enough to make them piping hot, and give them time to absorb all the flavours.

# TORTELLINI WITH CHEESE SAUCE

**H**ere is a very quick way of making a delicious cheese sauce without all the usual effort. But do eat it when really hot before the sauce starts to thicken.

### INGREDIENTS
*450g/1lb fresh tortellini*
*115g/4oz ricotta or cream cheese*
*60–90ml/4–6 tbsp milk*
*50g/2oz/½ cup grated St Paulin or*
*mozzarella cheese*
*50g/2oz/½ cup grated Parmesan cheese*
*2 garlic cloves, crushed*
*30ml/2 tbsp chopped fresh mixed herbs,*
*such as parsley, chives, basil or oregano,*
*and sprigs, to garnish*
*salt and ground black pepper*

### SERVES 4

1 Cook the pasta according to the manufacturer's instructions, in boiling, salted water, stirring occasionally.

2 Meanwhile, gently melt the ricotta or cream cheese with the milk in a large saucepan. When blended, stir in the St Paulin or mozzarella cheese, half of the Parmesan and the garlic and chopped herbs.

3 Drain the cooked pasta and add to the sauce. Stir well and cook gently for 1–2 minutes to melt the cheese. Season, and garnish with herb sprigs. Serve sprinkled with the remaining Parmesan cheese.

# PASTA WITH CHICK-PEA SAUCE

An unusual combination, the chick-peas give this pasta dish a delightful crunchiness. This is a quick, easy supper dish.

### INGREDIENTS

*5ml/1 tsp olive oil*
*1 small onion, finely chopped*
*1 garlic clove, crushed*
*1 celery stick, finely chopped*
*425g/15oz can chick-peas, drained*
*250ml/8fl oz/1 cup tomato sauce*
*225g/8oz pasta shapes*
*salt and ground black pepper*
*chopped fresh parsley, to garnish*

### SERVES 4

1 Heat the oil in a non-stick pan and sauté the onion, garlic and celery until softened but not browned. Stir in the chick-peas and the tomato sauce, then cover and simmer for about 15 minutes.

2 Cook the pasta in a large pan of boiling lightly salted water according to the manufacturer's instructions. Drain and toss with the sauce (*left*), then season to taste. Sprinkle with chopped fresh parsley and serve at once.

41

# PASTA WITH SPRING VEGETABLES

 nown as *pasta primavera*, this classic dish makes the most of fresh vegetables. For a lighter sauce, use Greek-style yogurt instead of the double cream.

### INGREDIENTS

*115g/4oz broccoli florets*
*115g/4oz baby leeks*
*225g/8oz asparagus*
*1 small fennel bulb*
*115g/4oz fresh or frozen peas*
*40g/1½ oz/3 tbsp butter*
*1 shallot, chopped*
*45ml/3 tbsp chopped fresh mixed herbs,*
*such as parsley, thyme and sage*
*300ml/½ pint/1¼ cups double cream*
*350g/12oz penne*
*salt and ground black pepper*
*freshly grated Parmesan cheese, to serve*

*SERVES 4*

1 Divide the broccoli florets into tiny sprigs. Cut the leeks and asparagus into 5cm/2in lengths. Trim the fennel bulb and remove any tough outer leaves. Cut into wedges, leaving the layers attached at the root ends so the pieces stay intact.

2 Cook each vegetable separately in boiling salted water until just tender – use the same water for each vegetable. Drain well and keep warm.

3 Melt the butter in a separate pan, add the chopped shallot and cook, stirring occasionally, until softened, but not browned. Stir in the herbs and cream and gently cook for a few minutes, until the sauce is slightly thickened.

4 Meanwhile, cook the pasta in boiling salted water for 10 minutes. Drain and add to the sauce with the vegetables. Toss and season with pepper.

5 Serve the pasta hot with a sprinkling of freshly grated Parmesan cheese.

# AUBERGINE LASAGNE

rich and filling supper dish that needs only to be served with a light green salad. It freezes very well.

### INGREDIENTS
*3 aubergines, sliced*
*75ml/5 tbsp olive oil*
*2 large onions, finely chopped*
*2 × 400g/14oz cans chopped tomatoes*
*5ml/1 tsp dried mixed herbs*
*2–3 garlic cloves, crushed*
*6 sheets fresh lasagne*
*salt and ground black pepper*
*fresh sage sprigs, to garnish*

### FOR THE CHEESE SAUCE
*25g/1oz/2 tbsp butter*
*25g/1oz/2 tbsp plain flour*
*300ml/½ pint/1¼ cups milk*
*2.5ml/½ tsp English mustard*
*115g/4oz/8 tbsp grated mature*
*Cheddar cheese*
*15g/½oz/1 tbsp grated Parmesan cheese*

*SERVES 4*

---

**COOK'S TIP**
To freeze, cook for only 20 minutes, cool, then freeze. Reheat at 190°C/375°F/ Gas 5 for 35-45 minutes.

1 Layer the sliced aubergine in a colander, sprinkling lightly with salt between each layer. Leave to stand for 1 hour, then rinse well and pat dry on kitchen paper.

2 Heat 60ml/4 tbsp of the oil in a large pan, fry the aubergine slices on both sides, then drain on kitchen paper. Add the remaining oil to the pan, cook the onions for 5 minutes, then stir in the tomatoes, herbs, garlic and seasoning. Bring to the boil and simmer, covered, for 30 minutes. Preheat the oven to 200°C/400°F/Gas 6.

3 Meanwhile, to make the cheese sauce, melt the butter in a pan, add the flour and cook for 1 minute, stirring. Gradually stir in the milk. Bring to the boil and simmer for 2 minutes. Remove from the heat and stir in the mustard and cheeses. Season.

4 Arrange half the aubergine slices in an ovenproof dish, add half the tomato sauce. Top with three sheets of lasagne. Repeat the layers. Add the cheese sauce, and bake for 30 minutes. Garnish with the sage sprigs and serve at once.

# GOLDEN VEGETABLE PAELLA

**W**ild rice is actually not a rice at all but a wild grass native to North America. It gives a nutty flavour and crunchy texture to this colourful dish.

### INGREDIENTS

*pinch of saffron strands or 5ml/1 tsp ground turmeric*
*750ml/1¼ pints/3⅔ cups hot vegetable stock*
*90ml/6 tbsp olive oil*
*2 large onions, sliced*
*3 garlic cloves, chopped*
*275g/10oz/1½ cups long grain rice*
*50g/2oz/⅓ cup wild rice*
*175g/6oz pumpkin or butternut squash, chopped*
*175g/6oz carrots, cut in matchsticks*
*1 yellow pepper, seeded and sliced*
*4 tomatoes, peeled and chopped*
*115g/4oz oyster mushrooms, quartered*
*salt and ground black pepper*
*strips of red, yellow and green pepper, to garnish*

### SERVES 4

1 Place the saffron, if using, in a small bowl with 45ml/3 tbsp of the hot vegetable stock. Stand for 5 minutes. Meanwhile, heat the oil in a large, heavy-based frying pan. Fry the onions and garlic for 2–3 minutes.

2 Add the rices and toss for 2–3 minutes until coated in oil. Add the remaining stock to the pan with the pumpkin or squash and the saffron strands and their liquid. or the turmeric. Stir as the mixture comes to the boil, then reduce the heat to very low. Cover the pan with a lid or foil and cook very gently for about 15 minutes. (Avoid stirring unnecessarily as this lets out the steam and moisture.)

3 Add the carrots, pepper, tomatoes and seasoning, replace the lid and cook over a gentle heat for a further 5 minutes, or until the rice is almost tender.

4 Add the oyster mushrooms, check the seasoning and cook, uncovered, for just long enough for the mushrooms to soften, without letting the paella stick. Top with the strips of pepper and serve at once.

# TAGLIATELLE WITH PEA SAUCE, ASPARAGUS AND BROAD BEANS

creamy pea and sage sauce combines wonderfully with the crunchy young vegetables in this light, summery pasta dish.

### INGREDIENTS
*15ml/1 tbsp olive oil*
*1 garlic clove, crushed*
*6 spring onions, sliced*
*225g/8oz/1 cup frozen petit pois, defrosted*
*350g/12oz fresh young asparagus*
*30ml/2 tbsp chopped fresh sage, plus extra leaves to garnish*
*finely grated rind of 2 lemons*
*450ml/¾ pint/1¾ cups vegetable stock or water*
*225g/8oz frozen broad beans, defrosted*
*450g/1lb tagliatelle*
*60ml/4 tbsp natural low-fat yogurt*

*SERVES 4*

1 Heat the oil in a pan. Add the garlic and spring onions and cook gently for 2–3 minutes until softened.

2 Add the peas, a third of the asparagus, the sage, lemon rind and stock or water. Bring to the boil, reduce the heat and simmer for 10 minutes, until tender. Process in a blender until smooth.

3 Meanwhile, remove the outer skins from the broad beans and discard. Cut the remaining asparagus into 5cm/2in lengths, discarding any tough fibrous stems, and blanch in boiling water for 2 minutes.

4 Cook the tagliatelle in a pan of boiling salted water for about 10 minutes until *al dente*. Drain well.

5 Add the cooked asparagus and skinned beans to the sauce and reheat. Stir in the yogurt. Add the sauce to the tagliatelle and toss together. Garnish with a few extra sage leaves and serve immediately.

# POLENTA AND BAKED TOMATOES

**A** staple of northern Italy, polenta is a nourishing, filling food, served here with a delicious fresh tomato and olive topping.

INGREDIENTS
*2 litres/3½ pints/8 cups water*
*500g/1¼lb quick-cook polenta*
*oil, for greasing*
*12 large ripe plum tomatoes, sliced*
*4 garlic cloves, thinly sliced*
*30ml/2 tbsp chopped fresh*
*oregano or marjoram*
*115g/4oz/1 cup black olives, stoned*
*salt and ground black pepper*
*30ml/2 tbsp olive oil*

SERVES 4–6

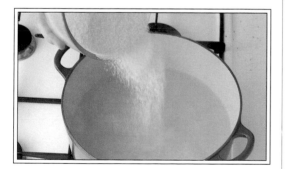

1 Pour the water into a large saucepan and bring to the boil. Add the polenta. Press out any lumps with a wooden spoon, then simmer for 5 minutes, until thickened.

2 Remove the pan from the heat and pour the polenta into a 23 × 33cm/9 × 13in Swiss roll tin. Smooth out the surface of the polenta with a palette knife until level, and leave to cool.

3 Preheat the oven to 180°C/350°F/Gas 4. With a 7.5cm/3in round pastry cutter, stamp out about 12 rounds of polenta. Remove the rounds from the Swiss roll tin with a palette knife and arrange them in a lightly oiled ovenproof dish so that they slightly overlap one another.

4 Layer the tomatoes, garlic, oregano or marjoram and olives on top of the polenta, seasoning the layers as you go. Sprinkle with the olive oil and bake uncovered for 30–35 minutes. Serve immediately.

# RICE WITH SEEDS AND SPICES

change from plain boiled rice, this dish is a flavourful accompaniment to serve with spicy curries. Basmati rice gives the best texture and flavour, but you can use ordinary long grain rice instead, if you prefer.

### INGREDIENTS
*5ml/1 tsp sunflower oil*
*2.5ml/½ tsp ground turmeric*
*6 cardamom pods, lightly crushed*
*5ml/1 tsp coriander seeds, lightly crushed*
*1 garlic clove, crushed*
*200g/7oz/1 cup basmati rice*
*400ml/14fl oz/1⅔ cups vegetable stock*
*120ml/4fl oz/½ cup natural yogurt*
*15ml/1 tbsp toasted sunflower seeds*
*15ml/1 tbsp toasted sesame seeds*
*salt and ground black pepper*
*fresh coriander sprigs, to garnish*

*SERVES 4*

1 Heat the oil in a large non-stick frying pan and add the tumeric, cardamom pods, crushed coriander seeds and garlic. Sauté for about 1 minute, stirring.

2 Add the rice and vegetable stock, bring to the boil, then cover and simmer for 15 minutes, or until just tender.

3 Stir in the yogurt and the toasted sunflower and sesame seeds. Adjust the seasoning and serve hot, garnished with the fresh coriander sprigs.

### COOK'S TIP
Seeds of every sort are particularly rich in minerals, so they are a good addition to all kinds of dishes. Light roasting improves their flavour.

# PENNE WITH BROCCOLI AND CHILLI

Make this spicy dish as mild or hot as you like by varying the amount of chilli. Slice the chillies finely so their heat spreads evenly through the dish.

### INGREDIENTS
*350g/12oz penne*
*450g/1lb broccoli, broken into small florets*
*30ml/2 tbsp vegetable stock*
*1 garlic clove, crushed*
*1 small red chilli, sliced, or 2.5ml/½ tsp chilli sauce*
*60ml/4 tbsp natural low-fat yogurt*
*30ml/2 tbsp toasted pine nuts or cashews*
*salt and ground black pepper*

### SERVES 4

1 Add the pasta to a pan of boiling salted water. Place the broccoli in a steamer over the top. Cover and cook for 8–10 minutes until both are just tender. Drain.

2 Pour the vegetable stock into a large saucepan and bring just to the boil. Add the crushed garlic and chilli or chilli sauce. Stir over a low heat for 2–3 minutes.

3 Stir the broccoli, pasta and yogurt into the spice mixture. Adjust the seasoning. Transfer to warmed individual plates, sprinkle with the nuts and serve immediately.

# TAGLIATELLE WITH HAZELNUT PESTO

For the health conscious, it is good news that hazelnuts are lower in fat than other nuts. In this recipe, they are used as an alternative to pine nuts in the pesto sauce.

### INGREDIENTS
*2 garlic cloves, crushed*
*25g/1oz/¼ cup fresh basil leaves*
*25g/1oz hazelnuts*
*200ml/7fl oz/⅞ cup low-fat soft cheese*
*225g/8oz dried tagliatelle, or*
*450g/1lb fresh tagliatelle*
*salt and ground black pepper*

### SERVES 4

1 Place the garlic, basil, hazelnuts and cheese in a food processor or blender and process to a thick paste or pound to a paste using a pestle and mortar.

2 Cook the tagliatelle in a large saucepan of lightly salted boiling water for about 10 minutes or until *al dente*. Drain the tagliatelle thoroughly.

3 Spoon the hazelnut pesto into the hot pasta, tossing until melted. Transfer to warmed individual plates, sprinkle with pepper and serve immediately.

# DEEP-PAN VEGETABLE PIZZA

A glorious mix of fresh vegetables tops this luxurious deep-pan pizza. Vary the vegetables according to what is in season, but aim for a variety of colours, shapes and textures.

INGREDIENTS
FOR THE PIZZA DOUGH
*175g/6oz/1½ cups plain flour*
*5ml/1 tsp salt*
*½ sachet easy-blend dried yeast*
*15ml/1 tbsp oil*
*about 120ml/4fl oz/½ cup warm water*

FOR THE TOPPING
*115g/4oz/½ cup canned*
*creamed mushrooms*
*50g/2oz each cooked French beans,*
*cauliflower florets and baby sweetcorn*
*6–8 cherry tomatoes, halved*
*2–3 pieces sun-dried tomato in oil,*
*finely chopped*
*30ml/2 tbsp ready-made*
*tomato sauce*
*50g/2oz/½ cup grated blue cheese*
*oil, for brushing*
*salt and ground black pepper*

SERVES 4

1 To make the pizza dough, mix together the flour, salt and yeast in a large bowl. Stir in the oil and enough water to mix to a soft dough. Knead for 5 minutes until smooth. Stretch out the dough and use to line an 18cm/7in deep pizza pan, or a shallow loose-based cake tin. Spread the pizza base with the mushrooms.

2 Arrange the cooked vegetables neatly over the top and sprinkle with seasoning. Add the halved tomatoes and the sun-dried tomatoes cut into tiny pieces.

3 Drizzle over the tomato sauce and sprinkle on the cheese. Brush with oil where necessary and sprinkle with more seasoning. Leave in a warm place for the dough to rise up to the top of the pan or tin.

4 Meanwhile, preheat the oven to 220°C/425°F/Gas 7. Bake the pizza for 15–20 minutes, until golden all over, bubbling in the middle and becoming quite crispy at the edges.

# PIZZA WITH FRESH VEGETABLES

T his pizza can be made with any combination of fresh seasonal vegetables. It is best to blanch or sauté them before baking.

### INGREDIENTS
*350g/12oz/3 cups plain flour*
*5ml/1 tsp salt*
*pinch of sugar*
*1 sachet easy-blend dried yeast*
*about 250ml/8fl oz/1 cup warm water*

### FOR THE TOPPING
*400g/14oz peeled plum tomatoes,*
*fresh or canned, drained*
*225g/8oz broccoli florets*
*225g/8oz fresh asparagus, cut into*
*2.5–4cm/1–1½in pieces*
*12 small courgettes, sliced lengthways*
*75ml/5 tbsp olive oil*
*50g/2oz/⅓ cup shelled peas,*
*fresh or frozen*
*4 spring onions, sliced*
*75g/3oz mozzarella cheese, diced*
*10 leaves fresh basil, torn into pieces*
*2 garlic cloves, finely chopped*
*salt and ground black pepper*

MAKES 4

1 To make the dough, sift the flour and salt and stir in the sugar and yeast. Add enough water to mix to a soft dough. Knead for 5 minutes. Cover and leave in a warm place for 1 hour, or until doubled in size.

2 To make the topping, strain the tomatoes through the medium holes of a food mill, scraping in all the pulp. Blanch the broccoli, asparagus and courgettes for 2–3 minutes. Drain well. Heat 30ml/ 2 tbsp of the oil, add the peas and spring onions and cook for about 5 minutes.

3 Preheat the oven to 240°C/475°F/Gas 9. Roll out the dough to make four 20cm/8in bases and place on baking sheets.

4 Spread the puréed tomatoes over the pizza bases, leaving the rims uncovered. Spread the other vegetables evenly over the tomatoes. Sprinkle with the mozzarella cheese, fresh basil, chopped garlic, salt and pepper and the remaining olive oil. Bake the pizzas for about 20 minutes, or until the crusts are golden brown, the vegetables are tender and the cheese has melted.

# CRACKED WHEAT WITH FENNEL

**C**ombining sweet and savoury flavours, this unusually crunchy salad is mixed with a delightful garlic vinaigrette dressing.

### INGREDIENTS

*115g/4oz/¾ cup cracked or bulgur wheat*
*1 large fennel bulb, finely chopped*
*115g/4oz French beans, chopped and blanched*
*1 small orange*
*1 garlic clove, crushed*
*30–45ml/2–3 tbsp sunflower oil*
*15ml/1 tbsp white wine vinegar*
*salt and ground black pepper*
*½ red or orange pepper, seeded and finely chopped, to garnish*

### SERVES 4

1 Place the cracked or bulgur wheat in a bowl and cover with boiling water. Leave for 10–15 minutes, stirring occasionally. When doubled in size, drain well and squeeze out any excess water.

2 While the wheat is still slightly warm, stir in the chopped fennel and the French beans. Finely grate the orange rind into a small bowl. Peel and segment the orange and stir into the salad.

3 Add the garlic, oil, vinegar and seasoning to the orange rind, and mix thoroughly. Pour over the salad and mix well. Chill the salad for about 1–2 hours, before serving garnished with the chopped pepper.

# CHILLED CHOCOLATE SLICE

**T**his is a very rich pudding, perfect for using up leftovers. You don't need to eat it all at once as it keeps extremely well.

### INGREDIENTS
*115g/4oz/½ cup butter, melted, plus*
*extra for greasing*
*225g/8oz ginger biscuits, finely crushed*
*50g/2oz stale sponge cake crumbs*
*60–75ml/4–5 tbsp orange juice*
*115g/4oz/½ cup stoned dates, warmed*
*25g/1oz/¼ cup finely chopped nuts*
*175g/6oz bitter chocolate*
*300ml/½ pint/1¼ cups whipping cream*
*grated chocolate and icing*
*sugar, to decorate*
*1 orange, cut into segments, to serve*

### SERVES 6–8

**1** Brush an 18cm/7in loose-bottomed flan tin with a little of the butter. Put the remaining butter into a bowl with the biscuit crumbs and mix together. Pack the crumb mixture evenly round the sides and base of the flan tin, pressing with the back of a spoon. Chill for 15 minutes while preparing the filling.

**2** Put the cake crumbs into a bowl with the orange juice and leave to soak. Mash the dates with a fork, add the cake crumbs and the chopped nuts and mix well.

**3** In a small pan, melt the bitter chocolate with 45–60ml/3–4 tbsp of the cream. Softly whip the remaining cream, then fold in the melted chocolate mixture.

**4** Stir the cream and chocolate mixture into the crumbs and mix well. Pour into the biscuit crust, mark into portions and leave to set. Scatter over the grated chocolate and dust with icing sugar. Cut into wedges and serve with the orange segments.

### COOK'S TIP
To make biscuit crumbs, either grind the biscuits in a food processor or a blender or place them in a strong plastic bag and crush them with a rolling pin.

# APPLE AND APRICOT CRUMBLE

ightly cook the fruit base first for the best results. That way you'll get a delicious contrast between the soft fruit and its crunchy topping.

### INGREDIENTS
*425g/15oz can apricot halves in natural juice*
*450g/1lb cooking apples, peeled and sliced*
*granulated sugar, to taste (optional)*
*grated rind of 1 orange*
*grated nutmeg, to taste*

### FOR THE TOPPING
*200g/7oz/1¾ cups plain flour*
*50g/2oz/½ cup rolled oats*
*150g/5oz/10 tbsp butter or sunflower margarine*
*50g/2oz/¼ cup soft brown sugar*
*demerara sugar, to sprinkle*

### SERVES 4–6

1 Preheat the oven to 190°C/375°F/Gas 5. Drain the apricot halves in a colander, reserving a little of the juice.

2 Put the sliced apples into a large saucepan and pour in a little of the reserved apricot juice and sugar to taste, if liked. Simmer gently for 5 minutes to cook the apple pieces lightly.

3 Transfer the apples to an ovenproof pie dish and add the apricot halves and orange rind. Add a little grated nutmeg to taste. Stir to combine the two fruits.

4 To make the topping, rub the flour, oats and butter or margarine together until they form fine crumbs. (You can use a food processor or blender if you prefer.) Mix in the soft brown sugar.

5 Scatter the crumble over the fruit, spreading it evenly. Sprinkle with a little demerara sugar. Bake for about 30 minutes, until golden and crisp on top. Allow the crumble to cool slightly before serving.

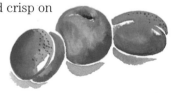

# SPICED PEARS IN CIDER

**A**ny variety of pear can be used for cooking, but firm pears are best for this recipe, as they do not break up easily – Beurré Bosc is a good choice.

### INGREDIENTS
*4 firm pears*
*250ml/8fl oz/1 cup dry cider*
*thinly pared strip of lemon rind*
*1 cinnamon stick*
*30ml/2 tbsp brown sugar*
*5ml/1 tsp arrowroot*
*15ml/1 tbsp cold water*
*ground cinnamon, to sprinkle*
*double cream, to serve (optional)*

### SERVES 4

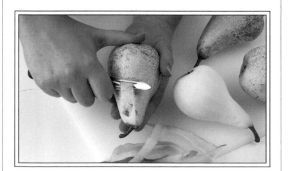

1 Peel the pears thinly, leaving them whole with the stems on. Place in a pan with the cider, lemon rind and cinnamon stick. Simmer for 15–20 minutes or until tender.

2 Lift out the pears. Boil the syrup, uncovered, to reduce it by about half. Remove the lemon rind and cinnamon stick, then stir in the sugar.

3 Mix the arrowroot with the water in a small bowl until smooth, then stir into the syrup (*right*). Bring the mixture to the boil and stir constantly over the heat until thickened and clear.

4 Pour the sauce over the pears and sprinkle with ground cinnamon. Leave to cool slightly, then serve warm, with double cream if you like.

# RASPBERRY AND PASSION FRUIT SWIRLS

**I**f passion fruit are not available, this simple dessert can be made with raspberries alone. Over-ripe, slightly soft raspberries can be used in this recipe.

### INGREDIENTS
*350g/12oz/2½ cups raspberries*
*2 passion fruit*
*225g/8oz/1⅔ cups low-fat fromage frais*
*30ml/2 tbsp sugar*
*raspberries and fresh mint sprigs,*
*to decorate*

### SERVES 4

1 Mash the raspberries in a bowl with a fork until the juice runs. Scoop the passion fruit pulp into a separate bowl, add the fromage frais and sugar and mix well.

2 Put alternate spoonfuls of the raspberry pulp and the fromage frais and passion fruit mixture into 4 stemmed glasses, or other serving glasses.

3 Stir lightly to create a swirled effect. Chill the desserts ready to serve. To decorate, place one whole raspberry and a sprig of fresh mint in the centre of each.

# APPLE AND MINT HAZELNUT SHORTCAKE

**A**pple and mint make an unusual filling for this nutty shortcake dessert but you can use any summer fruit, such as raspberries or strawberries, if you prefer.

### INGREDIENTS
*150g/5oz/1 cup wholemeal flour*
*50g/2oz/4 tbsp ground hazelnuts*
*50g/2oz/4 tbsp icing sugar, sifted*
*150g/5oz/10 tbsp unsalted butter*
*or margarine*
*flour, for rolling*
*3 sharp eating apples*
*5ml/1 tsp lemon juice*
*15–30ml/1–2 tbsp caster sugar, to taste*
*15ml/1 tbsp chopped fresh mint, or*
*5ml/1 tsp dried mint*
*250ml/8fl oz/1 cup whipping cream or*
*crème fraîche*
*few drops of vanilla essence*
*mint sprigs and whole hazelnuts,*
*to decorate*

*SERVES 8–10*

### COOK'S TIP
The shortcake bases can be made in advance, left to cool and stored for 7–10 days in an airtight tin.

1 Process the flour, hazelnuts and icing sugar with the butter in a food processor or blender in short bursts, or rub the butter into the dry ingredients until they come together. (Don't overwork the mixture.) Bring the dough together, adding a very little iced water if necessary. Knead the dough briefly, then wrap in greaseproof paper and chill for 30 minutes.

2 Preheat the oven to 160°C/325°F/Gas 3. Cut the dough in half and roll out each half, on a lightly floured surface, to an 18cm/7in round. Place on greaseproof paper on baking sheets and bake for about 40 minutes, or until crisp. If browning too much, move them down to a lower shelf in the oven. Allow to cool.

3 Peel, core and chop the apples into a bowl with the lemon juice. Transfer to a pan, add sugar to taste, then cook for 2–3 minutes, until just softening. Mash the apple gently with the mint and leave to cool.

4 Whip the cream or crème fraîche with the vanilla essence. Put one shortcake base on a serving plate. Spread half of the apple then half of the cream or crème fraîche on top. Place the second shortcake on top, then spread over the remaining apple and cream, swirling the top layer of cream gently. Decorate with mint sprigs and a few whole hazelnuts, then serve at once.

# INDEX

Apples: apple and apricot crumble, 58
  apple and mint hazelnut shortcake, 62
  apple, onion and Gruyère tart, 26
Apricots: apple and apricot crumble, 58
Artichokes: chick-peas and artichokes au gratin, 31
Asparagus: tagliatelle with pea sauce, asparagus and broad beans, 46
Aubergines: aubergine lasagne, 44
  baked aubergine slices, 22

Broad beans: tagliatelle with pea sauce, asparagus and broad beans, 46
Broccoli: broccoli and chestnut terrine, 30
  broccoli-cauliflower gratin, 32
  leek and broccoli tartlets, 20
  penne with broccoli and chilli, 50
  stir-fried florets with hazelnuts, 39

Carrots: lemon carrot salad, 34
Cauliflower: broccoli-cauliflower gratin, 32
  stir-fried florets with hazelnuts, 39

Cheese: apple, onion and Gruyère tart, 26
  baked aubergine slices, 22
  broccoli-cauliflower gratin, 32
  chick-peas and artichokes au gratin, 31
  leek and Stilton samosas, 14
  rice and cheese croquettes, 13
  spinach and ricotta conchiglie, 16
  tortellini with cheese sauce, 40
Chestnuts: broccoli and chestnut terrine, 30
Chick-peas: chick-peas and artichokes au gratin, 31
  Middle Eastern vegetable stew, 24
  pasta with chick-pea sauce, 41
Chilli: penne with broccoli and chilli, 50
Chocolate: chilled chocolate slice, 56
Cracked wheat with fennel, 55
Crisp fruity salad, 35
Curry: Thai tofu curry, 19

Fennel: cracked wheat with fennel, 55

Garlic baked tomatoes, 12

Hazelnuts: apple and mint hazelnut shortcake, 62
  stir-fried florets with hazelnuts, 39
  tagliatelle with hazelnut pesto, 51

Lasagne: aubergine lasagne, 44
Leeks: leek and broccoli tartlets, 20
  leek and Stilton samosas, 14
Lemon carrot salad, 34
Lentils: green lentils with sweet onions, 27
Middle Eastern vegetable stew, 24

Mushroom popovers, 28

Onions: apple, onion and Gruyère tart, 26
  green lentils with sweet onions, 27
Oranges: watercress and orange soup, 10

Passion fruit: raspberry and passion fruit swirls, 61
Pasta: aubergine lasagne, 44
  pasta with chick-pea sauce, 41
  pasta with spring vegetables, 42
  spinach and ricotta conchiglie, 16
Pears: spiced pears in cider, 60
Peas: tagliatelle with pea sauce, asparagus and broad beans, 46
Penne with broccoli and chilli, 50
Pizza: deep-pan vegetable pizza, 52
  pizza with fresh vegetables, 54
Polenta and baked tomatoes, 47
Potatoes: spicy baked potatoes, 38
  spinach and potato galette, 23
  watercress and potato salad, 36

Raspberry and passion fruit swirls, 61
Rice: golden vegetable paella, 45
  rice and cheese croquettes, 13
  rice with seeds and spices, 48
Salad: crisp fruity salad, 35
  lemon carrot salad, 34
  watercress and potato salad, 36
Spiced pears in cider, 60

Spinach: spinach and potato galette, 23
  spinach and ricotta conchiglie, 16

Tagliatelle: tagliatelle with hazelnut pesto, 51
  tagliatelle with pea sauce, asparagus and broad beans, 46
Tarts: apple, onion and Gruyère tart, 26
  leek and broccoli tartlets, 20
Terrine: broccoli and chestnut terrine, 30
Tofu: Thai tofu curry, 19
Tomatoes: baked aubergine slices, 22
  garlic baked tomatoes, 12
  polenta and baked tomatoes, 47
Tortellini with cheese sauce, 40

Vegetables: deep-pan vegetable pizza, 52
  golden vegetable paella, 45
  Middle Eastern vegetable stew, 24
  pizza with fresh vegetables, 54
Veggie burgers, 18

Watercress: watercress and orange soup, 10
  watercress and potato salad, 36

Yorkshire pudding: mushroom popovers, 28

Mushroom popovers, 28